STAFF TRAINING
A Librarian's Handbook

by

Margaret Blanksby

Newcastle-under-Lyme
AAL Publishing

The Association of Assistant Librarians
(Group of the Library Association)
acknowledge the assistance of REMPLOY
in the production of this publication

1988

12464

British Library Cataloguing in Publication Data
Blanksby, Margaret
Staff training: a librarian's handbook.
1. Library employees—Training of
I. Title
020,7,15   Z668.

ISBN 0-900092-68-8

CONTENTS

Page

Thanks—
to Pat for suggesting the writing and publication of the text
to Penny for typing
and
to John for reading the proofs.

FIGURES, EXHIBITS AND TABLES

1. Definitions

The primary reason for training is to enable an individual or a group to perform the required job to the required standard. A dictionary definition is "to bring to the standard, desired state or standard of efficiency by instruction and practice and to teach and accustom (the individual to do, to take action)". Therefore training is the process by which an individual learns new ways, information or techniques and changes from a state of being incapable of doing the job or being ineffective.

Training, as an event, occurence or activity, also includes applying the learning in practice. *Learning* can be described as knowing something that was not known before or being able to do something that could not be done previously—and being able to show them it. Thus learning can only be said to have taken place when it has been applied to the job.

Education is also a part of training as it is defined as the process of systematic instruction and development of knowledge. But as education mainly involves the background concepts, philosophies and underlying principles, education and training can not be used as synonymous terms. Education can be general; training must be job-specific (either to the present job or as development for future jobs). Kenny, Donnelly and Reid say "the objective of training is to assist a learner to acquire the behaviour necessary for effective work performance".[1]

Throughout the terms *"effective"* and *"efficient"* will be used to distinguish between doing the right things (so an effective performer is working at tasks which are intended to achieve the overall objective) and doing things right. The latter implies the performer may be working well but at a job which does not contribute to the objectives.

Behaviour—what an individual does or says—will be the main focus. For whilst attitudes can be learnt and do affect how an individual performs at work, they can be hidden, masked or feined. And as they are also formed from personal beliefs and personality they are not totally work concerns. How someone behaves is.

The word *"trainer"* will be used as a name for the provider or sponsor of a learning event. It does not mean the training officer nor the line manager. These people can be trainers, they can be other things as well, and peers or even subordinates can train. This is to distinguish between training—the task, and learning—the process, and to convey the notion that responsibility lies with everyone at work to be concerned with each other's training.

Thus the *trainee* is the individual who is or will experience the training event whilst the learner is part of the process of learning (though this does not necessarily mean they are receiving training). Again no hierarchical sense is implied. This is because learning is the process that enables change to happen and it can occur the many different ways—experience, contact with others, imitation and interpretation of others and by deduction. Every day can be a learning experience if the individual wants (or it can simply be a repeat of the previous day).

1

No-one can make an individual learn; they must want to. Thus attendance at a training course is not proof of learning. Every work encounter and experience can be used as an opportunity for learning which is not dependant on a training officer or line manager. Sometimes these serve to modify attitudes and behaviours; sometimes to reinforce existing patterns and beliefs. The impact of learning depends on the strength of influence and power possessed by the person encountered or the impact the experience has for the individual. The line manager can have a very positive or negative effect on helping the individual to learn and the opposite can be true. Likewise a colleague can be more influential than the boss or play no part at all. An experience can be glossed over and ignored or it can be remembered for the rest of the person's life.

Because learning can be powerful some means is needed to make sure that it is positive and effective. Unplanned or unfocused learning can be counter productive to efficient and effective performance and discourage future learning and development.

A *systematic approach* is the means of harnessing the individual's inherent curiosity, and their desire and ability to learn with the organisation's need for effective workers. It can be approached from two directions. One is aimed at an individual as a member of the work force with a need to be trained to do the job. The other is aimed at the individual with a need to be trained to meet existing performance requirements and to continue to learn to face new demands.

Both approaches are preparing for the future so the process of learning has to be continuous. Most of the diagrams in the text are circular as many of the under lying concepts in training are concerned with conveying a sense of continuity. The model of systematic training given in Figure 1 is no exception.

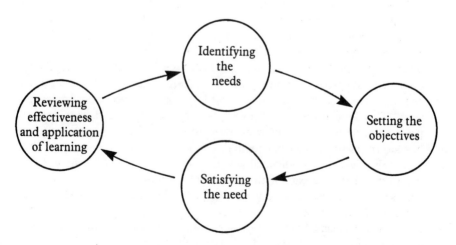

Figure 1—The Training Cycle. The systematic approach

Research[2] has shown that the most potent learning takes place when the individual is involved in setting the learning objectives and when reflection is encouraged. The individual learns best when they have the opportunity to influence the pace and style and when the purpose of the learning and its relevancy is clear to the individual.

The *"at work"* approach to training removes the need for the learning to be transferred. Its immediacy means that no effort is expended in trying to make the away from work learning fit into the every day context. It also means that the content can be controlled. The constraints of the organisation and the individuals are known and accounted for in the planning and execution of the activity.

However, using the everyday means that risks have to be taken by everyone involved—trainer, trainee and colleagues. The individual has to take risks by showing a lack of capability, appearing slow, asking questions, making mistakes and needing time and attention. The trainer needs to invest time and attention (and like any investment it contains chance), allow mistakes to happen and accept that the end result (an effective performer) is more important than the rigorous following of rules. They also have to be prepared to answer what may be challenging or uncomfortable questions. The answers to these may reveal better ways of doing the job or show the trainer's previous ideas or objectives as obsolete. Colleagues need patience, tolerance, to accept their responsibilities to help the trainer by giving support, feed back and encouragement and to recognise that they can not have as much time and attention from the trainer.

One responsibility of the line manager as part of their role is creating a *climate* where these risks can be taken. Another is to identify *true training needs* and a third is to give feedback. *Feedback* is a two way process essential for both—

for the trainer to check that the training is relevant (through the assessment of how effective and efficient the work performance of the trainee is compared to the standard required) and

for the trainee to know that the trials and tribulations of learning have been worth while, that progress and achievements have been made.

Training costs but it is an initial investment of time and energy which has to be balanced against the costs of poor, ineffective performance, errors and the under-realisation of potential. The systematic approach, if followed, should ensure the time/energy costs are minimal and the pay-offs great. Taking the risks to realise potential should, in the long term, increase the chances of organisational effectiveness and success.

REFERENCES

1 Kenney, J. Donnelly, E. and Reid, M. Manpower training and development: an introduction. 2nd Ed. 1979. I.P.M.

2 Reference should be made to the work of Reg Revans on action learning and the joint writing of Tom Boydell and Mike Pedler on self development for managers. The former in "Experiential learning" (Sheffield City Polytechnic 1976) says though, experiential learning is more than simply having experience of work—some means of reflecting on past and extending current experiences is needed.

2. Identification of Training Needs

The systematic approach to the identification of training needs has been described as focusing on organisational needs as its primary concern is to fit an individual or group of individuals to the job they are required to perform. Consequently the starting point is an outline of the job itself otherwise known as:

2.1 THE JOB DESCRIPTION

The job description specifies the general purpose of the job and gives the main duties and responsibilities the job holder will be expected to perform. It can be very specific, defining each duty in precise detail, or it can be very broad, leaving scope for interpretation.

The best examples outline the scope and constraints placed on the job holder whilst allowing room for some interpretation, flexibility and development. The clauses in the description should be behaviourally specific to give the individual and the organisation some measures for assessing performance.

Usually job descriptions are divided into three parts. The first gives factual information about the post title, grade, reporting lines, location etc. The second outlines the purpose or function and the third the duties and responsibilities. Exhibit 1 gives an indication of what can be included. The clauses have been designed to say what should be done by using active verbs, but how that action should be done is not specified to allow scope and flexibility.

2.2 PERSONNEL SPECIFICATION

The personnel specification builds on the job description. If the latter is the skeleton of the job holder (in performance terms) the specification adds the flesh. For it describes the qualities the person should possess for them to be effective. The specification is normally used in the selection process but it can also contribute to the identification of training needs by separating factors regarded as essential (ie those which the job holder should possess before taking up the appointment) and those which are desirable (ie those which can be acquired later). Exhibit 2 gives examples of the seven points normally used in personnel specifications.

2.3 TASK ANALYSIS

The job description can also be used to amplify the job in two other ways. The first, the task analysis, is shown as Exhibit 3. Here each component part of the job—the separate tasks—is broken down into individual stages that have to be completed for efficient performance. Each stage then is separated into steps. The third column in the analysis adds qualifying remarks.

2.4 **JOB SPECIFICATION**

The second way to use the job description is for the preparation of the job specification. Each task is taken and systematically divided into the knowledge, skill and attitudes needed by the job holder. The knowledge category is self-explanatory and may include such items as procedure, rules, principles and practices. The skills should be described in terms of behaviour, specifying what the individual will be required to do and what the skills are required to enable those actions to be made. Reference to Mager's[3, 4] books will provide useful assistance with this process. He recommends that objectives are described as performance (what can be done after training or instruction) carried out under specified conditions according to the laid down criteria (or standard). This may be over-rigorous for a normal job specification but his guidance helps to clarify an area that can easily be abstract and unprecise.[5]

The third part of the job specification is attitude. Attitudes are formed partially as a result of one's physical make-up and instinct but largely as a result of "education" and experiences. The education processes are the lessons taught by people with influence and those gained from experimentation in early life (pushing out the boundaries). Additionally messages are received, thought about, adapted and included into one's frame of reference throughout an individual's development. Thus attitudes are the values, beliefs, concepts that condition how one views the world. Some attitudes are very deeply held and some are superficial. But they do influence how an individual reacts or responds and the resultant action or behaviour. As attitudes are learnt they can be re-learnt, and as they influence behaviour at work they are legitimate areas of interest for the trainer. Attitudes are difficult to change, especially if they are deeply held. Individuals must have some reason to examine their existing value systems and be prepared to consider alternative view points. Trainees are unlikely to do this if the examination is done in a way that is dismissive or judgemental of their views or they are labelled as wrong. However, if they are helped to look at how their behaviour affects the job and how different behaviour would be more appropriate, a less threatening starting point can be found to begin the exploration. To do this the trainer needs to be able to describe the behaviour required. Mager (op. cit.) suggests using the indicators (what someone says or does) that suggest the "required" state of mind exists. An example of this would be:

"Thoroughness"—tasks completed within a reasonable timescale; attention paid to detail.[6]

Exhibit 4 shows the job specification further divided into levels of training:

Initial—what needs to be learnt immediately to perform the basic task.

Supplementary—what is needed to reach the state of an experienced and fully competent member of staff.

Developmental—what can be done to allow for the growth and improvement of the individual and the job. This is to create opportunities to realise the individual's potential whilst building on their ability to achieve the organisation's goals whilst contributing to their job satisfaction. At this level it is possible for diverse directions to be opened up so plans can only be general suggestions of possibilities rather than firm proposals.

and possible timescale for each level could be:

Initial—Months 1-6

Supplementary—Years 1 and 2

Developmental —Years 2 and 5

REFERENCES

3   Mager, R. Preparing instructional objectives. 2nd ed. 1986 and (4) Goal Analysis. 2nd Ed. Pitman Learning Inc.

4   Mager, R. and Pipe, P. Analysing performance problems. 2nd Ed. Pitman Learning Inc. 1984.

5   Mager, R. Preparing instructional objectives (op. cit.)

6   Mager, R. Goal analysis (op. cit.)

3. Faults and Performance Analysis

The systematic identification of training need focuses mainly on what is required to fit a new member of staff into an existing job. However this opportunity is increasingly less common and it is now more often a case of fitting an existing member of staff to a new (or changed) job. A systematic approach can be taken but as it is a very detailed and exhaustive process, quicker approaches may be more suitable. These given below focus on areas of current performance that either need to be changed if the job holder is to remain fully competent and effective or improved for them to meet new standards. This does not imply that staff are incapable or incompetent (even though in some cases this may be true) but recognises that as circumstances change new ways and methods need to be learnt. The approaches do not accept that all performance problems are due to or can be solved by training and suggest that other courses of action may be appropriate.

3.1 FAULTS ANALYSIS

This approach takes a problem, fault or failure of some kind and, by a series of structured questions, explores it. The questions are intended to separate causes from consequences and to recognise the immediate action that can be taken to resolve the fault and prevent its reccurance. The mneumonic is FACERAP and a worked example is given in Exhibit 5.

3.2 PERFORMANCE ANALYSIS

A full summary of this approach is given in Mager and Piper's book.[4] It is included as it explores the problem of poor or inadequate performance from several angles, some of which are normally not immediately obvious. It also recognises that training is one way of improving performance but others exist either to complement training or for independent use. It is more thorough than Faults Analysis and because of this only a brief example is given in Exhibit 6. Reference to the full text is recommended.

3.3 TRAINING AUDIT

Like any audit this technique allows a comparison to be made between the knowledge, skills and attitudes currently held and those needed for effective performance.

The two previous approaches focus primarily on the job holder, this one turns to organisational requirements by categorising training need into Administrative (or procedural) Technical and Human aspects. They can be more than training areas; they can be work areas needing adjustment or change. Exhibit 7 shows now an audit takes the current job and examines the aspects against training needs or areas to be changed.

4. Learning Objectives

The identification of need is the first part of the training process. This is shown in Figure 1. Before satisfactory means of meeting the needs can be found a statement of what the training is intended to achieve is required. This is usually given as a statement of aims and objectives. The aims describe what the training intends to cover in broad terms or content. The objectives specify what the trainee should know or be able to do when the training has been completed. Mager's[5] approach is helpful and provides the basis for the examples given in Exhibit 8.

The objectives firstly should describe what the trainee should know or be able to do in terms of action or behaviour. Thus "Have a good manner with users" or "have an appreciation of" are not adequate. Instead terms such as "Welcome users by saying good morning and smiling" or "able to explain accurately" are expressions of performance.

The second stage is to establish the standard of performance required; the criteria by which the trainee can be described as being acceptably competent. For example "maintaining accurate statistical records" requires that no mistakes should be made. Alternatively "filing 75% of all requests within one month" accepts that perfection is not always possible.

The third is to specify the conditions under which the performance and standard should be attained. This can be difficult; saying "under normal working conditions" seems to be the obvious condition—but what is normal? "Preparing time tables ensuring that two staff are on duty at all times" does not allow for unforeseen situations such as sickness. So a clause such as "using overtime or relief cover is allowed when staffing levels fall below those previously agreed".

The main purpose of an objective statement is for it to be helpful to both the recipient and the provider of the training—so that both know what has to be achieved and can recognise when that has or has not happened. But sometimes it is not possible or even desirable to be so precise about the required behaviour. Sometimes the performance has described in qualitative terms or as abstract concepts. An example of the latter is "good social skills". It is possible to recognise the obverse when they are observed but not so easy to describe their good use as a written learning objective.

Reference again to Mager[6] provides guidance. He suggests the question "How would you know one when you saw one" should be posed when trying to describe someone demonstrating the desired state or level of performance. The first stage is to specify what the trainees should do or say to demonstrate their achievement of the goal or desired state of competency. This can include behaviours that are or are not acceptable. Then add, as before, the standards and conditions to and under which the trainees will be expected to perform. As a learning objective the statement of a goal (or state of competency) is intended to be helpful and to be used as a means of informing the trainee what will be expected. Exhibit 9 illustrates the

11

"indicator" behaviours. It should be noted that straying into perfection is easy when describing the demonstration of attitude or the intangible, qualitative goals. If the goal analysis is to be helpful it has to be remembered that a state of perfection is unattainable—"stay within the zones of reasonableness".

5. Satisfying Training Needs (A)—Considerations

5.1 CLIMATE

For a trainee to put the training into practice and continue to learn from the job the working situation needs to be conducive. An easy statement to make but how can such a climate be established? It is commonly described as being risk free. But this can not be so, for if learning is about acquiring new knowledge or developing new skill, trying anything new involves taking risks. These risks include the admission of a lack of knowledge and skill, the chance that the learning will not be adequate and that failure will result. The transfer of training and application of learning always contains the risk of the unkown and the uncertainty of success.

The climate needs to allow these risks to be taken so the job can provide the opportunities for experiment and be conducive to try outs. It needs to be mistake tolerant and supportive. Support is given by acknowledging that mistakes are part of the learning process and opportunities are created for reflection on how the mistake happened and where additional improvement is needed. Only the same mistake repeated should cause concern. The climate should not be punishing to the individual until the reasons for the learning not being applied or not having been learnt properly have been investigated.

A climate conducive to learning is forward looking and positive. Everyday occurrences are vehicles for learning and development as they provide opportunities for appraisal. Appraisal means that individuals are able to check their progress individually or with peers or supervisor and a work group can appraise the achievement of their task. This appraisal gives the learner the information needed to assess progress and gain a sense of achievement whilst recognising areas for future development. At the same time work practices in need of improvement can be recognised. (Organisations learn as well as individuals). The trainer can check on the trainees' and the group's progress and take action to affect the changes and make provision for the additional learning.

A learning climate takes account of the individual's need for reasons to enable them to take the first risk (the acknowledgement of the need for training). This step sometimes is the most difficult as an admission of a lack (of knowledge, or skill or an inappropriate attitude) can be involved, even if it is only implicit. Regardless it has to be made.

Research[7] amongst Chief Executives has found that early jobs need to be challenging and stretching, with identifiable goals, which are not so hard to be demotivating. The ability to act independently with support and guidance is another requirement. The importance of practical experience, personal leadership from a trainer or supervisor, and the width of early experience recognised.

Ten factors that help establish a climate that encourages learning for the individual were found from these successful people.

1. Achievement of results
2. Work with a wide variety of people
3. Opportunity for challenge
4. Willingness and opportunity to take risks
5. Early responsibility for important tasks
6. Width of experience
7. Desire to seek new opportunities (and their provision)
8. Leadership
9. Ability (and encouragement) to develop ideas
10. Ability to change styles

Figure 2 shows other elements.

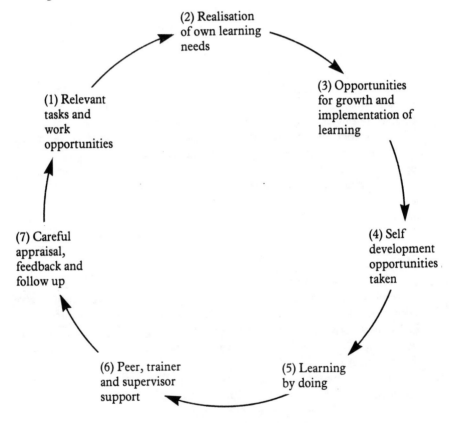

Figure 2—Elements of the Learning Climate.

5.2 THE LEARNER

Before deciding how training needs can be satisfied or what sort of learning opportunities can be stimulated, the trainer needs to take account of what the trainee already knows and is able to do. This can be assessed from the educational background and previous experience but as some assumptions have to be made caution is needed. The best way of gathering such information is to check with the trainee. In the case of attitude training assumptions are particularly dangerous as these can lead to prejudgement and stereotyping. Here again time taken to check with the learner can prevent waste and embarrassment caused by wrongly directed training or inappropriate contents.

5.3 LEARNING STYLES

Individuals have their own preferred style of learning and research has shown these preferences can speed or block the learning process. If the trainer is aware of the differences in style and chooses material and methods that suit those of the trainees the learning can be enhanced. If this consideration is ignored or the trainer's own preferred style determines the choice, without consideration of the trainees', their learning could be hindered.

Two research works have identified four predominate styles which can be used for guidance when choosing methods. They can be correlated:

Kolb's *Learning Style Inventory*[8]	Honey and Mumford's *Learning Style Questionnaire*[9]
Concrete Experience	Activist
Reflective Observation	Reflector
Abstract Conceptualisation	Theorist
Active Experimentation	Pragmatist

The very titles suggest the different preferences. For example someone whose preferred style is Activist will hardly take kindly to reading a lengthy text, neither will role play appeal to a Theorist.

Honey and Mumford have identified different types of job which attract individuals with similar styles but figures have not been recorded yet for library workers. Any trainer is advised to be aware of the learning style of their trainees both as a group and as individuals.

5.4 LEARNING SPEED

Another factor to be taken into account is the different speed at which people learn.

It would be easy for a trainer to conclude at this point that all training plans must be uniquely designed to fit each individual. This is not being advocated as the confines and limitations of organisations means that general approaches must be used—if only for reasons of cost and consistency. However, the trainer does need to take account of individual factors by being flexible—allowing for the slowest and the fastest, and adaptive—changing style or method if the trainee is not making the required progress at the expected rate.

5.5 RETENTION

The final variable is retention of information. Just as different individuals learn in different ways at different speeds, information is absorbed differently through the senses. This effects its reception and how well it is recalled. Figure 3 shows the importance of vision in relation to the other means of perceiving and receiving information. Research also suggests that the short-term memory is improved if a "message" is transmitted using visual aids. The following nursery rhyme supports this:

> I hear and I forget
> I see and I remember
> I do and I understand

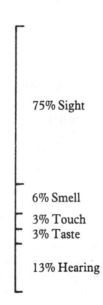

75% Sight

6% Smell

3% Touch

3% Taste

13% Hearing

Figure 3—Sensory Reception of Information

The importance of seeing and doing (especially the latter which will be discussed later) can not be over emphasised. Everyone can remember the pain and boredom caused by lectures given to an audience who have nothing to focus on or do except suffer hard chairs—who can remember the content?

The lesson for the trainer is to be mindful of attention time (20-40 minutes for one

16

means of learning), the need to use as many senses as possible and to vary the method and pace. But above all the learner should be given the opportunity to do. Figure 4 combines the variables. Once the initial stage of gathering information about the trainees is completed, differences in learning speed, absorption and retention should be accommodated-

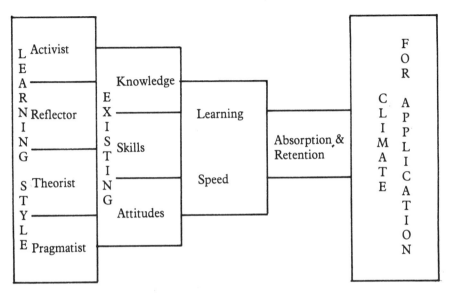

Figure 4—Variables in Learning

5.6 FACILITIES

The location in which the training is to take place should not dictate the choice of methods but its limitations need to be taken into account during their selection. Problems such as distraction, noise, interruptions, discomfort can all change what otherwise should have a successful event into a frustrating waste. Likewise the availability, useability and standard of equipment at the trainer's disposal can influence whether or not to use it. If the equipment is complex or unfamiliar or the state of repair dubious it may be better to leave well alone than risk the embarrassment incurred whilst trying to find out how to use or repair an essential machine in front of an audience.

5.7 PERSONAL LIMITATIONS

The trainer's own preferred learning style can be an influencing factor in the choice of method and design. There can be a tendency for a trainer to choose approaches that appeal to their own style. Additionally their own existing knowledge, skills and attitudes are helps and hinderances, just as they are to trainees. The trainer also is able to improve and grow. The satisfaction of others training and development needs can provide a vehicle for the trainer's learning.

REFERENCES

7. Journal of Management Development 4 (5) 1985. Margerison, C. and Kakabadse, A. What management development means for American CEO's.

8. Kolb, D. A. et al. Organisation psychology, an experiential approach. Prentice-Hall. 1974.

9. Honey, P. and Mumford, A. The Manual of learning Styles. Honey and Mumford. 1982.

6. Satisfying Training Needs
B—Methods

6.1 NOT A COURSE

Usually training is thought of as an off-the-job course, workshop or seminar run by a tutor with formal input being given by a lecturer. Participants are informed and directed. Whilst courses have their place they are only one way of meeting training needs. Sadly they are often regarded as being the only way and as such they become ends in themselves rather than the means. Also because courses are expensive and time consuming the cost can be prohibitive. This gives an excuse for not training in other ways.

Other methods are numerous and are grouped here into two categories for convenience. Some can be applied in either category and used at different stages in training and development. Variation in method helps to lengthen attention time and appeals to differences in learning style. In choosing a method the trainer needs to be conscious of the other constraints noted above and the influence of their own preferences.

The two categories are "Away from Work" and "At Work" and examples are given in Table 1. Research has demonstrated that the best way to learn about a job is by doing it—learning from experience. However simply learning by doing is not a satisfatory definition of experiential learning (see note 2 above). There needs to be the opportunity for the individual to reflect on past and extend current experiences to add to existing skills and knowledge. This is aimed at extending the ability to solve problems and to continue the learning about work and oneself. By using the work the training can be concerned directly with the current and future performance; it will provide opportunities for immediate feedback; the risks will be real and the learning relevant. It will have meaning to the individual and it will be personal—about how the person performs in the job. The individuals will have influence over the speed and pace, and the methods can be varied to appeal to their preferred style.

Kolb's four learning styles are formed into a cycle in Figure 5, as they also illustrate phases of the learning process in addition to style. As can be seen experience and experimentation are as important as reflection and conceptualisation. Away from work training accommodates preferences and need to reflect and conceptualise by providing the opportunities to stand back from the everyday. But the nearest they can get to experience and experimentation is through simulations and role play. (These are often criticised for their lack of realism.) On the other hand there are ways creating opportunities for reflection and conceptualisation to take place at work.

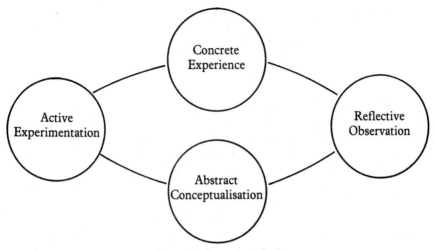

Figure 5—Learning Cycle

When looking for means of satisfying training needs the first place a trainer can seek opportunities is in the job itself. Advantages additional to those for the learning process include cheapness, relevancy, trainer/trainee control and, no need to replace lost time. One frustrating spin off from training is the inability, for whatever reason, to make use of learning. At work training reduces the transfer time required to translate away from work learning into the context of the job. Learning at work allows the trainee to know that it will be of value and will be useable immediately.

Table 1—At and Away from Work Training Activities

AT WORK	AWAY FROM WORK
Within job	
—expanded assignments (eg tasks, projects, investigations, reports)	—courses, seminars, conferences, workshops
—attendance at meetings,	—extra-job experiences
—training sessions	eg professional meetings
—performance review	meetings with other agencies
—coaching	—voluntary, civic, social, community,
—making presentations to meetings & training sessions	political activities
—writing reports	—in authority activities (eg social union, work groups)
—exposure to higher levels of management & specialists	—planned & guided reading
—career coaching and structured development rotations, plans	
—job enrichment & enlargement schemes	

20

On top of Job

—sick leave, maternity, holiday cover
—assisting manager with tasks &
  projects
—publicity work
—involvement in community or
  inter-agency groups
—special assignments (eg task force,
  project group membership,
  research, membership of
  committees and working parties)
—problem solving tasks

Special Arrangements

—job exchange
—secondments
—temporary promotion
—special assignment to senior managers

6.2 AT WORK OPPORTUNITIES

a) Planned Training Activities

These activities (plans and programmes) can make use of at and away from work activities for all stages in development.

Exhibit 10 shows part of the training programme for a library assistant during their first year in the job. These and programmes for other staff (not shown) cumulate into the plan. A plan shows how the longer term needs of the individual or group will be met. Exhibit 11 gives an example for a community library.

For any planned activity preparation is crucial for its success or failure. It requires time and thought but the expenditure of effort outlaid is an investment which will be repaid. (The cost of training staff to perform to the required standard is far less than the later cost of rectifying mistakes or dealing with a poor performer). Sadly preparation is often neglected—possibly because of the cost, the over confidence of the trainer, the apparent lack of time or simply lack of knowledge of its importance. A preparation checklist includes items such as:

  — *Who* (trainer and trainee's existing knowledge, skills etc)
  — *Where* (location, equipment)
  — *What* (content—in context, in a logical sequence, in chunks large
    enough to be meaningful, small enough to be absorbed
  —*Aids and materials* (available, pertinent up to standard)

21

b) Unplanned Training Activities

Obviously these activities can not be prepared in the same way for, by their very nature, they are opportunistic. But as the opportunities are in themselves, predictable some forward planning can be done so that best use can be made of them when they arise.

For example, a new member of staff is following an initial basic tasks programme. Some training is being done at work with the individual being instructed in some of the routines. Reading in the shape of the staff manual has been given and attendance at internal courses has been arranged. As part of the section the member of staff attends the monthly staff meetings. These meetings are divided into two sections—matters of business and discussion on a theme or area of work. The member of staff is making good progress—is there any need for more training?

One function of unplanned activities is to enhance the planned training by creating opportunities to explore an interest or concept further; to look at how a job has been done and how it could be done better; to take advantage of a new situation by using it as an investigation or a challenge. The trainer giving the new member of staff a journal article on the topic of the last meeting and suggesting that it be discussed, is training.

Another example would be for the trainer to observe the trainee dealing with a query and to ask (immediately afterwards and if possible not in public) how the trainee thought they had handled it—how the questions had been framed, what sources used—in effect what was good and what could be improved.

Delegation is another example of unplanned training and development. Giving a trainee whole responsibility for a project or investigation can involve the individual in new areas of work and at the same time as giving a sense of responsibility and maybe increased job satisfaction. Projects and investigations sound very grand but they can include simple, everyday activities such as a user survey to find the cheapest but most acceptable brand of coffee for the staff room; looking at the arrangement of the work rotas and gaining agreement to changes; building up relationships with specific teachers in the local school and helping to plan the class work for the next year.

The trainer and trainee can change roles in unplanned training as the trainer can also learn. Naive questions (like why) asked during discussions can stretch the trainer's thinking and stimulate their learning. In a learning environment there are no experts, no masters, only others with different experiences, knowledge and skills. Everyone can contribute, from their own point, and become equal partners in learning. This is possible when everyday is seen as being an opportunity for growth.

Mistakes present the opportunity to identify weaknesses and strengths and, with the aid of diagnostic tools such as FACERAP, can draw attention to areas that need improvement or change. In a learning climate they are not opportunities for allocating blame and punishment. New demands and situations need not be threats. (The chinese symbol for change means dangerous opportunity.) What better description for a chance to learn.

6.3 AWAY FROM WORK ACTIVITIES

The main advantages of at work training revolve around the immediacy and relevancy of the content, the multiplicity of opportunities and the ability to create a learning climate made up of learning colleagues. Away from work activities have disadvantages. These include cost, transfer of the learning and the time away from the job. Time is also needed to build relationships with other learners to develop the trust required for risks to be taken and attitudes to be explored.

The advantages come from the contact with other people not normally met and the exploration of atternative ideas and ways of working. Having the space and time to consider and think away from everyday problems and pressures is another major advantage.

The Preparation Checklist can be expanded as the need for good preparation is common to all activities. (See Table 1)

1 Who—is going to conduct the activity; do they have the necessary information about the trainees; does the "Who" have adequate knowledge of the content and the necessary presentation skills; does the "Who" know about the training need and the constraints on implementing learning; how much confidence does the trainee have in the "Who"; how much influence does the sponsor have over the content?

2 Where—is the location adequate regarding comfort, temperature, quiet, facilities, refreshments, equipment, atmospherics etc; how far do the trainees have to travel (is the journey "easy"); are the joining instructions clear and informative; if it is not to standard are there any alternatives; is the venue the most economical.

3 What—how relevant is the content; will it have meaning and interest to the trainees; will it be implementable; is the content in logical sequences; is it pitched at the right level; how much influence do the sponsor and trainees have over the content; can it be adapted if necessary, can it be transmitted better in a shorter space of time.

4 Aids and Materials—is the right equipment available; does the trainer know how to use it; is it adequately maintained; are the aids appropriate and relevant.

   —Is the material relevant, is the standard adequate; are all documents ready and available.

The problem of transferability deserves particular mention. Learning requires effort on behalf of the learner. The inability to transfer or use that learning is a major source of frustration that can devalue training and can cause major disillusionment. Problems occur when the course content is esoteric—interesting but too remote to be applicable. Or when the working situation does not allow the learning to be put into practice. This last point can be caused by a host of factors but needs to be considered when sponsoring an individual on an away from work training event.

The costs of training also require consideration. These can be described as being direct and hidden and can include

Direct	*Hidden*
a) location costs	a) opportunity costs
b) materials & equipment	—what would the trainer and
c) trainer fees	trainee be doing otherwise
d) salaries for staff cover	b) cost—benefits
or replacement	—what would not doing the
e) travel expenditure and	training cost versus the
subsistence	direct cost
f) administration costs	—what will be done better as a
	result of training
	c) other hidden costs include
	overhead and employment costs.
	These can be twice the
	individual's salary

Having considered all the factors the trainer can then decide whether an away from work event is valid or whether a more appropriate means of satisfying the training need exists.

6.4 COACHING AND COUNSELLING

Coaching and counselling are mentioned separately as they are both techniques that can be used at or away from work, in a planned or opportunistic fashion. Often the terms are used synomously, in fact they are different ways of approaching two distinct situations.

Coaching is when an individual is given aid, encouragement and support by another more skilled or knowledgeable in a particular activity. The technique is concerned with improving the coachee's competency and capabilities. The coach can use haphazard occurrences (such as an angry user) by taking the event quickly after it has happened and talking through it with the coachee. The latter will be encouraged to reflect on how the situation was handled and how that contributed to the outcome—satisfactory or otherwise. The coachee will be asked to consider what went well and what went not so well, what improvements could be made and how the outcome would have been different if another approach had been used. A coaching session can be held around case studies, using a group discussion as a means of throwing up different approaches for debate. The coachee(s) are then encouraged to try out the alternatives as a means of improving their performance. The coaching session can be conducted at work, with the coach working alongside the coachee, demonstrating alternatives and discussing the outcomes there and then. Alternatively, the session can be held in the workroom, away from interruptions to give the coachee the opportunity to reflect and explore, possibly, sensitive areas. So the difficult customer handled poorly, instead of being a bruising memory, becomes a learning opportunity with the member of staff receiving practical guidance on how the situation can be used to improve the way users are treated.

Counselling is different in so much as the technique is used when a problem (discrepancy between the present and the desired performance) exists. Examples can include performance problems (eg lack of attention to detail when filing) inappropriate attitudes (eg off-hand treatment of users) or some kind of personal problem that is affecting their work. The counsellor's role is to help the individual sort out what the "real" problem is, to recognise that it is their problem and to work out ways for themselves to resolve or minimise the problem. The second phase is to give the individual encouragement and feedback during the implementation of the "solutions".

Further information on these techniques is available from the Local Government Training Board or by reference to texts such as Singer.[10] No more will be said here as the techniques require skill as well as knowledge if they are to be used effectively. Reference to the sources were recommended.

6.5 SELF LEARNING

So far, most concentration has been given to training as an activity or opportunity initiated by a "trainer", outside the control of the trainees. If training is going to meet its objectives the trainee must learn (ie know something that was not previously known or do something that could not previously be done *and* show it). The trainee must want to learn and must have access to the resources needed to enable the knowledge or skills to be acquired. These resources do not have to be supplied by anyone else—some are available from within the individual. The training must be of interest or of meaning for the individuals for them to expend the energy and effort needed for the acquisition. If the training is always external the learners may not want any learning to take place.

Research has borne out the need for the learner to have a large element of control over what is to be learnt and how the learning will take place. Action learning is an established means of meeting this need (see foot note 2) and some approaches to self-development start by encouraging the participants to identify what they need to learn to achieve their personal goals. The Open University's approach and many correspondence courses try to build in flexibility in addition to meeting this need. The development of open and distance learning embrace these principles also.

Advances in computer-technology enable a personalised approach to be taken. The individuals can identify their needs and match into a data base which provides a uniquely designed programme. The most sophisticated packages base the training material on an interactive computer/video programme. The package is designed to allow the learner to retrack and review, thus allowing for differences in learning speeds, and employs different methods within itself (eg text, film clips, question and answers, testing etc). Obviously, this approach is high cost and machine dependant but its versatility is advantageous as it allows the learner to be in control.

The developments in self and distance learning include the computer based packages mentioned above and other examples of how efforts are being made to "free" the trainee from the trainer can be found amongst the "correspondence" courses now available (eg Open University, Open Polytechnic, Open Business School, NALGO/BTEC's Public Administration Certification. Newcastle Polytechnic's package on statistics etc). They use advanced technology of some kind even if it is only tape recording and can be costly. The approach and underlying concepts however can be scaled down. All libraries are stocked with the records of mankind's knowledge which were the main sources for Everyman's self learning. It has been mentioned before everyday can be used to try out other ways of doing the job and acquire skills. The learner can be encouraged to reflect and learn from those experiences: Rodin's "Thinker" did not need a computer.

6.6 TRAINING METHODS AND AIDS

Exhibit 11 shows that several different methods can be used easily in-house. These and others are outlined below. The need for preparation will be stressed again as it is cost-effective Failure to prepare can waste the opportunity. Several of these methods can be merged to give variety to a session or programme or can be self-contained for shorter sessions.

Instruction—"I do it normal, I do it slow. You do it with me, off you go". A task or routine is demonstrated, placed in the context of the whole job, the trainee is given time to practice, feedback on progress is given, the trainee is encouraged and rewarded for achievement. This is the most common way of introducing a new task that requires skill for effective performance. Often called "sitting by Nellie" it is dependent on Nellie's skills. The three main reasons for failure are—lack of preparation; trying to pack too much into one session and failure to train Nellie in the instruction techniques. Video Arts training film[11] demonstrates these skills.

Demonstrations—A mass version of the above. This is done for example by the supplier of new equipment. The main problems associated with this technique are location, size of audience and lack of opportunity to try out. Too large an audience and a poor location will restrict the amount an individual can see or hear and limit the chance to try out in the demonstrator's presence. Alternatively a demonstration to a small number of "Nellies" who then instruct the rest is a cost-effective way of using external expertise.

Lecture—An individual gives formal imput to an audience followed by the opportunity for questions or discussion. It is best used for the transmission of information. Consideration needs to be given to attention time and the use of visual aids. Size of audience will influence the quality of any subsequent discussion Large audiences can inhibit individuals or can lead to a series of disjointed questions and answers.

Seminar—An "expert" meets with a small group of trainees to discuss a topic in depth. Good for understanding policies and areas where attitudes influence performance.

Workshop—Group of trainees with similar needs and interests are brought together, with instructors, trainers or specialists as resources, to work through a topic. This can be conceptual for knowledge and understanding or practical for skill development. Cases, simulations, role play or real projects can be used.

Discussion Groups—Groups of individuals come together to talk through a topic of mutual concern. The success of this method is dependant on the skill of the leader. These include the ability to draw in low level contributors, preventing those with higher levels from dominating and keeping the discussion positive and forward moving. It is possible for discussion leaders to develop skills to distinguish between Process (what is going on in the group that helps or hinders its working) and Task (the nuts and bolts of running a discussion).

Forum or Panel Discussion—Two or more "experts" are brought together to debate a topic in front of an audience. This method is a good way of airing controversial views and exploring a problem area in depth. Opportunities for questions can be provided if appropriate.

Course—A course is a programme of study/learning. The content is structured towards specific learning objectives and, as it is trainer-centred, the trainees are expected to fit their needs to the course on offer. It is mainly used for the acquisition of knowledge but does not exclude skill development or exploration of attitudes.

Conference—An opportunity for individuals to gather to exchange views on areas of common interest. Often the exchange takes place outside the formal sessions which use other methods to explore specific areas. It is common to hear participants say the main value is in the informal conversations rather than the sessions. (One must question why it is so common to have pre-arranged workshops, lectures or seminars, why not facilitate discussion groups comprised of those with mutual interests.)

Visits—Tours and visits to other work sites are not an uncommon way of introducing other work methods or widening trainees' knowledge of other activities. The method can be enhanced by a pre-visit discussion on what can be expected to be gained and a follow-up or review of the visit. Location and size of audience can detract from such a visit so reading matter is a useful way to augment the information transmitted. The skills of the individuals conducting the tour can also influence quality. But preparatory and follow-up work can diminish any negative impact caused by these.

Case Studies, Simulations, Role Plays—are contrived situations, based on real life that give the trainee the opportunity to experiment in a low-risk setting. They can be run for an individual or a group. Case studies are intended to illustrate

27

principles, simulations develop problem solving abilities and role plays provide opportunities for developing skills by practicing them.

Critical Incidents—take an occurrence and by exploring the build up, the event and its consequences, use real life as a vehicle for learning and improving on performance. This approach can be used for individual coaching or with a group as a review.

Projects, Task Forces—These methods employ a real piece of work to provide the experience of planning and implementing a defined task and working with others. Projects can be individual, which gives added responsibility, but they require additional support from the trainer. Groupworking can provide this support but introduces the need to be aware of the dynamics of groups.

Programme Texts—The cheaper version of computer based learning. It does not have as much scope for variety as its high tech cousin but it employs the same principles. Learners are able to progress at their own pace and the opportunities to review and check understanding and reasoning are created. Trainees are asked to read a text and to answer a multi-choice question. Depending on which answer is chosen the individuals move on or are either referred back or sent to another section for additional explanation. Progress can be assessed and a sense of achievement gained. Trainee are able to work through the programme alone, in spare slots of time. Mager's text on objectives (op cit) uses this method and the currently popular fantasy books give an example of on the theme variation.

Manuals—Every library must have one! Either for rules and regulations or set procedures. They can gather dust or be very useful training aids: this is dependant on the skill of the author, the contents and the presentation. These are dependant on the manual's purpose. The manual can be a guide to policy and be used to aid interpretation or it can lay down rigidly prescribed rules, legislating for every eventuality, to be followed to the letter.

The job of the author is to write clearly what is required so that the reader is not left in doubt. The training package "Put it into writing"[12] gives advice on writing in general and the Plain English Campaign also gives some useful tips.

The contents are dictated by the purpose but they must be relevant to those who are going to use the manual. The way the contents are presented should be designed to help understanding. A narrative can be complex and difficult to follow in an emergency, whilst a flow chart can be absorbed quickly. Alternatively a chart with a lot of different routes can be convoluted. Additionally consideration needs to be given to how the manual is to be kept up to date.

A well produced staff manual that is fit for its purpose can be a valuable training aid as well as giving necessary information. Anyone considering going into production is referred to Morrel's text.[13]

Tests—can be used to check comprehension, knowledge or skill. They can be used to identify training needs or, by using pre and post tests, to check on the success of the training. They need careful construction to ensure that the real interest areas are being tested and the means of testing are legitimate and valid. Misleading or trick questions will not check a trainee's knowledge nor will the trainer be trusted for long.

Guided Reading—This approach is cheap and easy and can provide valuable background to concepts and principles. It would be a mistake however to assume that because a trainee works in a library that they are literate and are able to learn by reading. Before expending vast sums on books and journal articles it is worth checking an individual's learning style.

Check Lists—Exhibit 12 gives an abstract from a basic task check list. It is a useful aide memoire for the trainer and allows the trainee to see where they are going. It gives a sense of achievement and provides a record of what has been covered. The usefulness is dependant on the trainer being skilled in one to one training and being conversant with everything in the check list. Presentation can be important as well. A massive document can be very off putting to a new starter, whilst an attractive document can be an encouragement.

Technology Based Methods—Slides, tapes, audio visual presentations, films and videos have been grouped together. Firstly they are expensive and secondly, unless they are produced to a very high professional standard, they can be disastrous as aids to learning. They are expensive in terms of production, facilities and equipment needed for their use and unless they have been specifically commissioned they need to be translated for local use. They also become dated very quickly. People, generally, are exposed to high quality audio-visual material on the television, in the cinema and at exhibitions—anything less can look amateurish. Tony Jay[14] gives excellent guidance in his book and says "what is being communicated is still what matters. The medium is not the message. The medium is the envelope, and you are concerned with the letter inside. You should worry if Marshall McLuhan collects envelopes." In other words if the message doesn't need audio-visuals leave well alone; if it does at least consult with the professions.

Structured Group Learning—This method has been kept until the end as it merits longer explanation than those preceeding as it is not often cited in training texts. It has been used to good effect, especially for topics that could otherwise be deadly boring. The two variations are described briefly below but as it is not possible to give full details here, anyone wishing to make use of this approach is urged to make contact with the Local Government Training Board.[15]

a) Shared Group Learning—This is particularly useful when a lot of detailed information needs to be absorbed and a high level of understanding attained. The trainees are given a text which they are asked to study in detail. They then complete a multi-choice questionnaire based on the text before the training session. The first part of the session is spent in small groups comparing answers to the questionnaire and agreeing a consensus answer to each question. Reaching consensus is an important part in gaining understanding, as the participants explore each others reasoning and clarify different interpretations of the text. The arrival at a consensus decision—which may still be wrong—is learning in itself as the participants have to eliminate disagreement through debate rather than voting, trading or weight of numbers.

During the second part of the session the correct answers are disclosed and the reason for their correctness given. Full explanation is essential as by this stage the participants will have invested time and energy into the final group decisions and deserve the rationale.

The third phase is experimenting with the implementation of the learning using case studies and group discussion. This allows understanding to be checked and possible problems to be worked through.

This method has been used successfully in situations where new legislation has been enacted, where a complex concept had to be transmitted and where complicated routines were being introduced.

b) Shared Group Teaching—The group of trainees is split into sub-groups or individuals. Each is allocated a section of the "lesson". They are sent out to investigate that area and return to the larger group to share their learning.

The two approaches have been combined to liven up an orientation programme. Instead of visits to sections the participants were given an introductory text outlining the department's history and purpose. At the end of the first sharing session each participant was asked to choose a service (eg services to children). They were then allowed two weeks to approach staff active in the area and gather information about what and how the services were being provided. At the end of the second sharing session a back up document was given. This was a safety net to make sure the participants had all the information the department wanted them to have. The staff taking part were very enthusiastic about the approach. Shared group teaching has also been used to compare how different companies dealt with users during a public relations course.

To conclude this section on methods and aids the following the principles governing their selection are given:
— The method should be chosen according to its efficiency and effectiveness in satisfying training needs.
— The KISS (Keep it simple, stupid) principle should apply.
— The temptation of using methods because they appeal to the trainer should be avoided.
— Preparation needs to be done thoroughly and systematically.
— An aid should add to the message not detract.

Methods and aids are the tools in the trainer's tool bag, they are means to the end. Not the end—The end is what the trainee has learnt.

REFERENCES

Local Government Training Board, Arndale House, Arndale Centre, Luton LU1 2TS.

10. Singer, E. J. Effective Management Coaching. 2nd ed. IMP. 1979.

11. Video Arts—"You'll soon get the hang of it"—Training Film/Video and booklet.

12. Joseph, Albert. "Put it in writing", Training Films International 1982.

13. Morrell, J. C. Preparing an organisation manual. Institute of Management Foundation. 1977.

14. Jay, A. An Effective Presentation. B.I.M. 1970.

15. Local Government Training Board, Arndale House, Arndale Centre, Luton LU1 2TS

7. Evaluation of the Trainee and the Training

The Glossary of Training Terms[16] states that evaluation is "the assessment of the total value of a training system, course or programme in social as well as financial terms." Evaluation differs from validation as it attempts to assess the overall cost benefit of the course programme not just the achievement of its laid down objectives. The term is also used in the sense of the continuous monitoring of a programme or of the training function as a whole. "Validation is internal—a series of tests and assessments designed to ascertain whether a programme has achieved its specified behavioural objectives and external—the behavioural objectives of an internally valid programme were realistically based on an accurate initial identification of training needs in relation to the criteria of effectiveness adopted by the organisation."[15]

Figure 6 shows the different levels of validation and evaluation in the context of the organisational objectives.

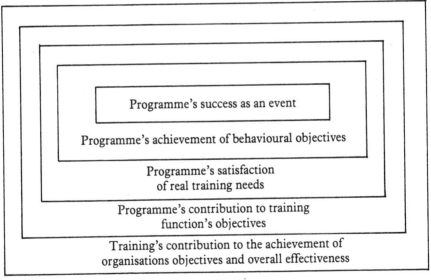

Figure 6—Levels of Validation and Evaluation

Several stages can be identified in the process of validation and evaluation. These, in a way, parallel the systematic training cycle and are pre-requisite if the process is to have any true meaning to the trainee, trainer and organisation.

These stages comprise of:
(a) setting performance standards and measures
(b) appraisal of performance (validation)
(c) giving feedback
(d) evaluating the performance
and Figure 7 shows the parallels.

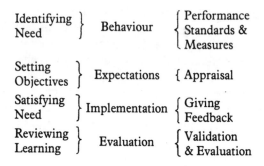

Figure 7—Identification and Evaluation of Training Need

7.1 PERFORMANCE STANDARDS AND MEASURES

These are particularly important and need to be behaviourally specific so the setting of learning objectives can be as mentioned above. The training then can be assessed and the trainees will know what is expected of them. This need becomes a necessity when assessing whether the trainee is applying the learning and performing to the required standard on the job.

If the primary function of training is to contribute to the whole organisation's effectiveness by enabling the trainees to pass from a state of ignorance and incapability to a state of being a fully competent and effective members of staff, the organisation and the individuals need to know what is a fully competent and effective member of staff.

Management by Objectives and a complimentary technique were developed as a means of marrying objectives (in terms of performance, outputs and achievements) with the behaviours and standards needed to attain them. The approach attracted a lot of criticism but it can be argued that the shortcoming were as a result of poor implementation rather than being integral to the technique. Mb0 is intended to allow staff to participate in the establishment of goals and objectives for their section. The process requires the objectives to be defined in terms of their contribution to the total organisation and allows the person who established them to have sufficient authority for their realisation and achievement.

The short-comings of Mb0 in practice have been because objectives were set in vague, unmeasurable terms, targets were set so low that they were meaningless or too high to be unachievable, or they were unrelated to the real job. Other short-comings are found when managers pay lip service to the need for staff to be truly involved in the establishment of the objectives, the staff not being given the authority to achieve the targets and poor feedback being given.

The complimentary technique is Behaviourally Anchored Rating Scales. BARS are constructed from specific examples of behaviour that indicate levels of performance in very much the same sense as Mager's "How would you know one when you saw one". Once the important elements and extreme levels of performance have been identified they are used as the anchor points on which rate performance. 6 to 10 elements of the job are normally specified. The process of identifying the elements and extremes can include the staff of the section. Thus the evaluation of performance can be rated on specific behaviours that are related to the job and are meaningful to the staff being evaluated.

Exhibit 13 shows how an objective can be used to elicit the indicator behaviours. These then can be used to rate the level of performance of an individual trainee and assess their progress over time. The Mb0 and BARS statement can also be used as a statement of training and development needs and learning objectives.

7.2 PERFORMANCE APPRAISAL

Some organisations find it useful to develop a system to formalise the appraisal and evaluation of an individual's performance. The purpose behind such a system is to assess the standard of performance achieved (and maintained), effectiveness of training and future training and development needs. Some systems are tied to payment or promotion and some to development and progress.

The system can be formalised into a structured assessment scheme, relying on forms and pre-arranged interviews. It can be a semi-formal regular discussion held between manager and staff individually as a matter of course without needing a formal, organisation wide scheme. But regardless of whether the system is formal or an approach by an individual manager there is a need for staff to be given feed-back on their performance. Staff have a right to that feedback and for it to be given skilfully, in a way designed to help them learn, develop and progress.

Without feed-back trainees will make their own assessment of how well they are performing. This could be an accurate assessment, or the trainees may over or under estimate their standard. If individuals have invested in learning they have a right to know whether it has been a positive contribution to the organisation. Similarly the organisation needs to know that its investment in its staff is paying off and that the staff are developing their effectiveness.

A systematic approach (be it formal or informal) can help to reduce subjectivity and value based judgements. Making use of techniques such as Mb0 and BARS also helps. A forward looking approach, using the past as a vehicle for learning for the future can avoid a punitive critical review of the provision year. Gerry Randell[17] and friends have developed an approach they call "Active Staff Appraisal" and suggest ways of making the assessment of performance into an opportunity to plan future development. Figure 8 presents a diagramatic representation of the process and draws attention to the features that define its purpose.

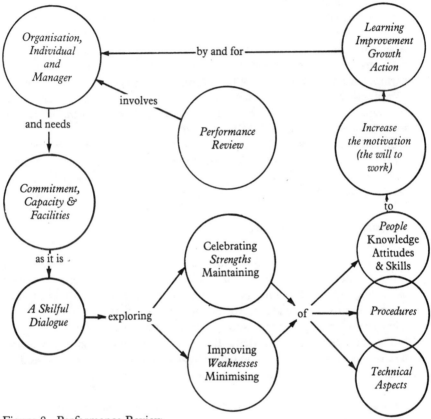

Figure 8—Performance Review

7.3 **GIVING FEEDBACK**

Giving feedback is a skilled process that can be learnt and improved upon. It is not easy, especially if the feedback is not good and because of this it is often avoided. But avoiding giving feedback can eventually result in more difficult situations that have to be addressed later. For example if a poor performer over-estimates their standard of performance and the performance is condoned for several years it becomes nearly impossible to take corrective action. Giving useful feedback earlier may eventually be easier and certainly fairer to the individual concerned and their colleagues.

Like many skilled processes there are guidelines which can be learnt and practised to make the job easier. These are given below in Exhibit 14. In addition consideration should be paid to when the feedback is to be given and the location (and its layout) where the discussion is to take place.

7.4 VALIDATION AND EVALUATION OF TRAINING

a) Internally—Was the training successful as an event—did the method and approach work?—were the behavioural objectives achieved?

b) Externally—Did the training satisfy "Real" training needs—were the objectives those required by the organisation? Are the staff increasing in competence?

c) Did the event contribute to the achievement of the training function's objectives—is there a consistency in how the different events come together to enable the role of training to be a positive contribution.

d) Is the training function contributing to the organisation by helping it become more effective—are staff developing and maintaining the organisation's ability to adapt and respond?

The above are some of the questions stemming from Figure 6 that need to be answered when validating and evaluating any separate training activity. Figure 1 shows the place of evaluation in the cycle and its primary function is to permit the feedback to have influence on the next stage of identifying new or additional training needs. Unfortunately the cycle is a closed loop, which if it remains unbroken, can spin in isolation without having any meaning. This is a criticism that training attracts. Evaluation can break this cycle by providing the means of answering the questions and ensuring that training is closely allied to the organisation's objectives.

The most common means of evaluating training events is by a questionnaire. As courses tend to be the most frequently used training method post course questionnaires (or happiness sheets) will not be unfamiliar. The term happiness sheet is used disparagingly as the questionnaires are usually distributed at the end of a course and are completed during the euphoric days following. The questions commonly focus on venue, food, method of presentation, quality of materials and visual aids, tutor style and degree of participation. These cover the first part of (a) and questions on whether the course achieved its objectives and met expectations go some way towards (b). But they do not ask what has been learnt as new knowledge or what can be done as a result.

Post-course questionnaires do have a value in the validation of training, but they need to be carefully designed and not relied on solely. Exhibit 15 gives an example of such a questionnaire aimed at eliciting the trainees' views. There is always the danger of the trainees writing what they think is expected of them or saying what the trainer wants to hear. The exhibited version is designed to be used for any training event, not just courses.

A more exhaustive approach is to ask the first two questions before the event and then match pre and post-event questionnaires. By including the views of the sponsor the validation moves towards full evaluation. A fuller approach would be to obtain the sponsor's reasons for initiating or supporting the training, and the trainee's motivation for participating. Both their expectations and their views about the impact of the training in meeting those needs could they then be sought. The contribution to the trainees and the organisations effectiveness could be acquired later. Instead of giving out questionnaires at the end, a more accurate assessment can be made by delaying a short while. This allows the euphoria to diminish and for the training to be seen more in the context of everyday realities by both the trainee and sponsor.

Similar approaches include pre and post training testing and observation. These are particularly useful for checking on the acquisition of knowledge and skills. A questionnaire is stronger on the exploration of attitudes. Tests and observation schedules need to be designed with the same rigor as questionnaires to ensure that the right areas are being covered.

These approaches to validation and evaluation are time consuming and costly and one must question the cost effectiveness of the process. Is it better to ensure that current activities are being done right or to spend the time assessing and satisfying new needs? The answer has to be a balance. One way of achieving that is by checking the Training Function's contribution to the overall effectiveness of the organisation. Periodic discussions with senior staff, training sponsors and trainees to review and explore the whole range of past activities and those that will affect future training needs monitors the total effectiveness of the training.

So by balancing the micro

—each training and development event

with the macro

—satisfying training and development needs and increasing the level of effective performance

in the context of the meta

—the organisation's objectives,

the training cycle ceases to be a closed loop and becomes an ever changing, developing growth process that helps an organisation respond and adapt. This is seen in Figure 9.

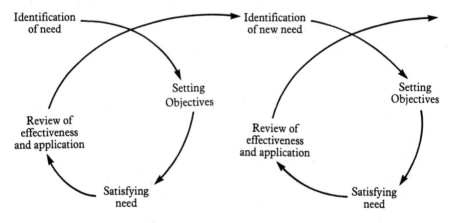

Figure 9—The growth process

16. Department of Employment (M.S.C.) Glossary of Training Terms. 2nd Ed. H.M.S.O. 1981.
17. Randell, G. Packard, P. and Slater, J. Staff Appraisal: a first stop to effective leadership. I.P.M. 1984.

8. Conclusion

Organisational effectiveness, in terms of a community library, has been defined as its ability to put people first (providing a service orientated towards satisfying their needs.) As people's needs are for ever changing a community library must be able to adapt and change so it can continue to respond to new needs. (The alternative is to take a stop-start approach—defining the needs and service and continuing along that path until some trauma requires a change and redefinition of need).

An adaptive, responsive organisation is made up of people who possess the same attributes. Training and development can contribute to the acquisition of those attributes. It can reflect the stop-start process by laying down precisely what someone needs to do. Or it can contribute to a climate where everyone is an equal learning partner. That is being:—

— able to identify learning needs in the context of the organisation's objectives
— able to take responsibility for one's own learning
— able to take responsibility for helping each other

The systematic approach advocated in the text aims to help the reader find ways of satisfying the organisation's needs with those of the learner by creating a climate for development. The individual's responsibility is for themselves alone.

The examples in the text are for illustrative purposes only and need to be adapted to meet local circumstances. They attempt to balance the need for staff to be competent at the prescribed job with that of giving the trainees scope to become equipped with the skills that will enable them to grow. They also are intended to illustrate that training doesn't need a large budget or a training officer. Training is the responsibility of all (especially the line manager) and most of it can be done everyday at work.

9. Additional Reading

In addition to the texts quoted in the foot notes the following are commended.

Belbin, E and Belbin, R M
Problems in adult retraining
Heinemann.

Boydell, T H
A guide to the identification of training needs and
A guide to job analysis
BACIE 1979

Castelyn, M
Planning library training programmes
Andre Deutsch. 1981

Conry, B
Library staff development and continuing education
Libraries Unlimited Inc. 1978

Day, H
Self instruction: an approach to staff training
HMSO 1984.

10. Exhibits

EXHIBIT 1—JOB DESCRIPTION

Post Title: Community Librarian
Grade: SO1
Reporting to: Assistant County Librarian
Responsible for: Assistant Community Librarians and Senior Library Assistants
Location: South Area

Job Purpose:
1. To organise, co-ordinate and develop library services and activities within the Area.
2. To be responsible for the general standard of service provision within the Area.
3. To contribute to the development and appraisal of departmental policies.
4. To liaise between the department and members of the community.

Duties/Responsibilities:

1. Community
   a) To promote the library service and activities and to encourage their use by all members of the community including groups and organisations, children and adults.
   b) To develop and maintain community profiles for information and to help to develop services and activities to meet specific needs.
   c) To identify priorities and areas of special needs.

2. Stock and Services
   a) To select and maintain stock and materials to reflect the community's needs and interests.
   b) To maintain the condition of the stock.
   c) To provide and develop information services to complement those provided by other agencies to ensure the community's information needs are met.
   d) To monitor and appraise the use made of the services with the participation of staff and members of the community, recommending and implementing changes as appropriate.

3. Staff
   a) To manage the staff of the area, supervising their effective deployment and working arrangements to provide an effective service.
   b) To be involved in the selection, promotion and transfer of staff.
   c) To provide training and development opportunities for staff and to participate in the department's training activities.
   d) To assess staff's performance in conjunction with the requirements of the Performance Review Procedures.

4. Building and Equipment
   a) To report on the state of repair of buildings and equipment and to order repairs within the agreed budgets and procedures.
   b) To encourage and provide for the use of buildings and equipment by community groups in accordance with policy.
   c) To be responsible for the safety and security of the buildings and contents.
   d) To contribute to the study and application of new technology.

5. Miscellaneous
   a) To prepare reports and statistics.
   b) To attend meetings.
   c) To contribute to publications.
   d) To take responsibility for safe and healthy working as defined by policy.
   e) To keep up-to-date with professional affairs and developments.
   f) To undertake any other duties and responsibilities which do not change the character and purpose of the post as requested.

EXHIBIT 2—PERSONNEL SPECIFICATION

Post—Community Librarian

Points	Essential	Desirable
1. Physical Make-up eg health and physical conditions, speech and appearance	Speech clear and verbal communication understandable	"Normal" standard of health
2. Attainments a) Education	Library Qualification and eligibility for full membership of a recognised relevant association.	Management qualification
b) Experience	Public library work.	Management or supervisory
3. Intelligence (used to distinguish between what someone has done from what they say they could do)	Ability to sustain a conversation at different levels (from transmission of simple information to a conceptual topic)	Ability to perform complex calculations and handle several projects at one time
4. Special aptitudes (specific for the particular job)	Ability to run and speak to public meetings	To speak to a conversational standard in at least one of the languages found in the community
5. Interests (intellectual, practical, constructional, physical, social, artistic etc)	Not applicable	An interest in working with young people. Some artistic talent
6. Disposition (How acceptable is the job holder to others)	Evidence of social skills Willingness to work as part of a team	Ability to work alone if required
7. Circumstances (only include those that affect the job)	Willingness to work irregular hours	Driving license

EXHIBIT 3—TASK ANALYSIS

To maintain the condition of the stock

Stages	Steps	Remarks
1. Stock Revision	1. Examine all stock	including loan records
	2. Identify community interests	
	3. Identify gaps in holdings or subjects inadequately covered due to lack of stock or out of date stock	be aware of new interest areas including non-book sources
	4. Search for suitable publications	including non-book sources
	5. Select and order	remain within budget
2. Stock Condition	1. Examine shelf stock to check physical condition and up to dateness	see 1-3 above
	2. Identify stock for repair, rebind, replacement or discard	within policy
	3. Organise for repair or rebinding	within budget
	4. Select and order for replacement	within budget
	5. Discard	Check for last copy status

EXHIBIT 4—JOB SPECIFICATION

a. To develop and maintain community profiles for information; and
b. To help to develop services and activities to meet specific needs.

Knowledge	Skills	Attitudes
Initial		
a. 1. Reasons for community profiling	1. Interpersonal and social skills	1. Thoroughness
2. Principles and techniques of community profiling	2. Search and enquiry skills	2. Accuracy
3. Data collection techniques	3. Questioning and listening skills	3. Diligence
4. Sources of community information	4. Questionnaire compilation	4. Self motivation
5. Data storage and retrieval methods	5. Surveying skills	
6. Limitations and constraints on choices and sources, techniques and methods		
b. 1. Types of services and activities able to be provided and existing within system	1. Interpersonal skills	1. Helpfulness
2. Categories and definitions of specific needs		2. Responsiveness
		3. Adaptability
Supplematary		
a. 1. Statistical methods	1. Analytical and numerical skills	1. Accuracy
2. Alternative means of data storage including an appreciation of computer applications	2. Problem solving	2. Flexibility
3. Non-traditional sources of information	3. Decision making	3. Appreciation and understanding of goals and priorities
4. Goals and priorities of system	4. Setting and adjusting priorities	4. Ability to put them into perspective
b. 1. Means and ways of developing contacts in the community and with agencies within and without Library	1. Interpersonal skill	1. Open Mindness
2. Knowledge and understanding of role	2. Public speaking	
3. Awareness of limits of authority	3. Consultative and participative skills	
4. Constraints upon means of responding to needs	4. Communications	
	5. Working with and motivating others	
Developmental		
1. Others information needs	1. To make use of community profile in other ways	1. Openness
2. Ways and means of adjusting existing services and activities to meet changing needs (including knowing how to achieve organisational change)	2. Influencing skills	2. Adaptability
	3. Negotiating skills	3. Learningful
	4. Interpersonal and social skills	4. Self motivation
3. Knowledge of techniques and methods used by similar, related professions (eg community development)	5. Communication skills	5. Enthusiasm
		6. Clarity of vision for Library and own goals
4. Ways of consulting and encouraging participation by community in service development		7. Participative and sharing

EXHIBIT 5—FAULTS ANALYSIS

Failure to compile Area Profile

Ascertained 1. Required document not produced
2. Preliminary data gathering not started

Caused 1. Failure to appreciate the need
2. Different priorities
3. Does not know:
   a) how to compile a profile
   b) how to collect data
   c) where to obtain data
4. Lacks confidence needed to obtain data from others

Effect 1. Service and meeting needs of community (falling issues, work level indicators for stock, registered borrowers falling)
2. Bookstock issue turnover declining
3. Increasing use of neighbouring libraries
4. Increasing complaints
5. Increasing requests for material from other service points

Responsibility 1. Community Librarian
2. Line Manager

Action Line Manager to explore the questions listed under Causes.
For 1 and 2 check knowledge and understanding of policies and priorities and, if needs be, arrange for coaching/counselling.
For 3 arrange for knowledge/training.
For 4 arrange skills/assertiveness training and provide back-up support and follow-up.

Prevention Line Managers to a) ensure that policies and priorities are known and understood by all staff,
b) check that basic training is provided to supply the necessary knowledge and skills so that staff know how and are able to perform all required tasks to the desired standard,
c) monitor and hold discussions with staff to check confidence levels,
d) be aware of failure to perform to required standard early so that corrective action can be taken before the problem becomes entrenched.

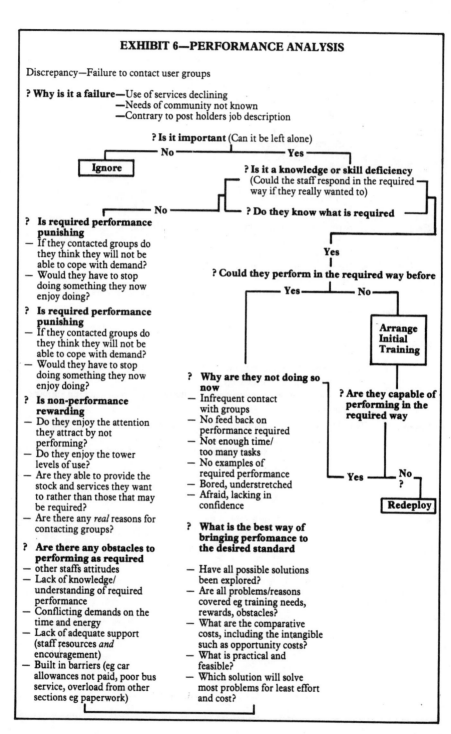

EXHIBIT 6—PERFORMANCE ANALYSIS

Discrepancy—Failure to contact user groups

? Why is it a failure—Use of services declining
—Needs of community not known
—Contrary to post holders job description

? Is it important (Can it be left alone)

No — **Ignore**

Yes — **? Is it a knowledge or skill deficiency** (Could the staff respond in the required way if they really wanted to)

No — **? Do they know what is required**

Yes — **? Could they perform in the required way before**

Yes / No — **Arrange Initial Training**

? Is required performance punishing
— If they contacted groups do they think they will not be able to cope with demand?
— Would they have to stop doing something they now enjoy doing?

? Is required performance punishing
— If they contacted groups do they think they will not be able to cope with demand?
— Would they have to stop doing something they now enjoy doing?

? Is non-performance rewarding
— Do they enjoy the attention they attract by not performing?
— Do they enjoy the tower levels of use?
— Are they able to provide the stock and services they want to rather than those that may be required?
— Are there any *real* reasons for contacting groups?

? Are there any obstacles to performing as required
— other staffs attitudes
— Lack of knowledge/ understanding of required performance
— Conflicting demands on the time and energy
— Lack of adequate support (staff resources *and* encouragement)
— Built in barriers (eg car allowances not paid, poor bus service, overload from other sections eg paperwork)

? Why are they not doing so now
— Infrequent contact with groups
— No feed back on performance required
— Not enough time/ too many tasks
— No examples of required performance
— Bored, understretched
— Afraid, lacking in confidence

? What is the best way of bringing performance to the desired standard

— Have all possible solutions been explored?
— Are all problems/reasons covered eg training needs, rewards, obstacles?
— What are the comparative costs, including the intangible such as opportunity costs?
— What is practical and feasible?
— Which solution will solve most problems for least effort and cost?

? Are they capable of performing in the required way

Yes / No ?

Redeploy

48

EXHIBIT 7—TRAINING AUDIT

Existing performance— Avoids speaking at public meetings
Required performance— Required to give short presentations to user groups outlining services and activities of Department and local library

KNOWLEDGE	SKILLS	ATTITUDES
Administrative		
1. Requirement of job to give such presentations		Perspective and understanding of policy requirements
2. Policy regarding which groups to approach	Adaption of policy constraints into practice	Willingness to interpret policies into practical delivery of service
3. Policy regarding contents of presentation		
4. Knowledge of services and activities		
5. Knowledge of existence of groups		
Technical		
1. Methods of presentation	public speaking and presentation	Self confidence, approachable out going, flexible
2. Methods of approaching groups and promotion of service	Skills (including preparation of promotional literature and personal contact)	
3. Awareness of different approaches needed for different groups	Communication skills	
Human		
1. Knowledge of others needs	Social skills, ability to judge audience reactions	Sensitive Adaptive
2. Appreciation of attention time		

EXHIBIT 8—LEARNING OBJECTIVE

a) *Request Procedure*

Following basic training the library assistant will be able to fill in the request form,

(PERFORMANCE)

completing each section accurately,

(STANDARD)

after having confirmed the bibliographic details by fully checked the catalogue and British Books in Print

(CONDITIONS)

b) *Fire Procedure*

All members of staff, when asked,
will be able to describe

(PERFORMANCE)

accurately

(STANDARD)

the procedure for implementing the fire/emergency procedure and put it into practice correctly and quickly during a drill or in a real emergency.

(PERFORMANCE, STANDARD and CONDITION)

EXHIBIT 9—GOAL ANALYSIS

For the description of attitude or competency—"Good social skills".

How would I know one when I saw one? (ie what indicator behaviours would be displayed by someone with good social skills and by someone with bad social skills)

"Good"	"Bad"
Smiles at users	Is abrupt
Greets users by saying a welcoming phrase	Continues desk work
Stops desk work	Avoids eye contact
Listens and asks questions	Does not check on understanding of request
Takes user to shelves	Points to shelves
Checks on understanding of request	Does not follow up to check user satisfaction
Suggests alternatives	Does not notice user's hesitance
Checks on suitability of material	
Checks users knowledge of issue procedures	
Asks if any more assistance is needed	
Concludes exchange with a pleasantry	

Standard —Always when working with users of the service
(Any drop in standard should be followed up by line manager)

Conditions —When on public service duty and when working in public areas

EXHIBIT 10—TRAINING PROGRAMME FOR A NEW LIBRARY ASSISTANT

WORKING AREA	TRAINING NEEDS	HOW TO BE MET	WHEN Weeks	BY WHOM
A. Induction	Following induction check list for domestic arrangements. Simple work routines on counter with attached L A. Discussions with key individuals when not on counter.	Attachment to experienced Library Assistant. Meetings with key individuals. Senior & Children's Library Asst., Community Librarian, Director/Deputy, Shop Steward	1	Meeting
B. Service Routines 1. General counter Duties	Routines of issue, and discharge of all materials. Separation of returned stock into shelving and those in need of attention. Shelving routines and sequences.	Instruction at the counter	1–2	Senior Library Assistant
2. Registration	Registration procedure, categories of membership. Principles of free libraries	Instruction in procedure, Explanation and discussion in work room	6	Senior Library Assistant
3. Requests	a) Request procedure. b) Use of catalogues and bibliographic tools. c) Explanation of inter-library co-operation.	a) Instruction on counter b) Instruction in Bibliographic Unit b & c) Attendance at Internal short course	8 12–26 26	a) LA in charge of requests b) SLA Bibliographic Services c) Training Section
4. Enquiries	Question technique, Knowledge of services and sources	Attendance at internal short course or in-branch seminar	18–26	Head Info. Services Community Librarian
5. Telephone	Answering, Taking messages, Enquiry work	a) Demonstration at counter and discussion in work room. b) Attendance at internal short courses	2–4 12–26	a) Senior Library Assistant b) Training Section

6. Complaints	Procedures, Byelaws and Regulations, Assertion Techniques	a) Attendance at internal short course b) Demonstration and instruction at counter. c) Demonstration in workroom.	16—26	a) Training Section b) Senior Library c) Assistant
7. Handling Cash	a) Use of till, b) Charging Policies, c) Accounting procedure	c) Discussion in Admin. Attachment to experienced Library Assistant. Meetings	4	a) & b) Senior Library Assistant c) Admin. Officer
C. Services to user groups	Introduction to concept of user group approach Attachment to one user group specialist	Internal short course/Discussion with Community Services Librarian/ Community Librarian	26—36	Training Section SLA or Self
		Internal short course/seminar Visit with user group Specialist/Attendance at meetings	30—40	Training Section Self & Specialist
D. User Education	Reasons for user education a) Involvement in preparing for groups, observation of sessions. b) Methods of presentation. c) Observed conduct of sessions	a) Discussion with User Education Librarian/Community Librarian. b) Internal short course. c) Coached by Community Librarian	40 / 40—52	a) Self & User Ed. Librarian. b) Training Section c) Community Librarian
E. Display Work	Reasons for display and promotion a) Types of work that can be done. b) Planned work with other library staff c) Preparation and mounting a display	Internal short course a) Community Librarian b) Visits to other libraries graphics unit and work with SLA and others Coached by SLA	26—36 / 30—40	Training Section a) Self & Community Librarian b) Self, Other libraries c) Graphics Unit Senior Library Asst.

53

EXHIBIT 11—TRAINING PLAN
FOR NEUVILLE BRANCH

WHEN	WHAT	HOW	WHO
SEPTEMBER	New start induction a) General Counter Duties b) Library Association Conference	Attachment and meetings Instruction and coaching for new start Conference	A Smith Susan L A Jones C Leela Patel
OCTOBER	a) Telephone Work b) Registration procedure c) "Developing relationships with schools" d) Handling cash e) Cash procedures	Demonstration & staff meeting Instruction for new start Department workshop Demonstration & staff meeting Instruction for new start	Susan L A Jones and British Telecom SLAJ School Section Admin Officer SLAJ
NOVEMBER	a) Bonfire night display b) Request work c) Staff supervision	Coaching in display work New start to work with New start to visit Internal short course	Graphics Section Lucy Adams SLA Biblio- graphic Services Training Section Andy C L Baker & Personnel Dept.
DECEMBER	a) Services to the retired b) Activities for Christmas c) Training on supplying requests	Staff meeting seminar Coaching and review of activities projects Internal short course	CLP & user group specialist Staff involved with CLP Training Section
JANUARY	a) Complaints — Review of those received in last 6 months b) Handling difficult customers c) Skills of assertion d) Community profiling e) How to use statistics	Staff meeting (Revision of procedures) Internal short course Authority short course Department seminar Internal short course	SLAJ New start & Linda Adams Training Section Personnel & New start CLP & ACLB Training Section SLAJ
FEBRUARY	a) "Questions and Answers" (Enquiry work) b) Developments in information services c) Annual development discussions	Internal short course Staff meeting Discussion	New start & Head (Information services) SLAJ & SLA (Info.) CLP and all staff

EXHIBIT 12—BASIC TASKS CHECK LIST

TASK 4.4 To answer simple enquiries and provide information	Comments	Completed Trainee	Trainer
a) How to answer enquiries	Augmented by short course attendance		
b) Sources of information —location in service point —how to use each source	Short course attendance See also (k)		
c) How to refer enquiries			
d) How to find contact points in other agencies	Internal directory		
e) What to do if the enquiry can not be answered			
f) What to do if the enquiry is "suspect"	Staff Manual entry		
g) How to record enquiries	Staff Manual entry		
h) How to reply to enquiries that have been left	telephone technique and letter writing courses		
i) Use of enquiries index			
j) Importance of checking up-to-dateness and accuracy	Short course attendance		
k) Contacting external agencies	as (c) and (h)		
l) Policy on charging for costs incurred (eg telephone data base costs, photocopies)	Staff Manual entry		

EXHIBIT 13

An Mb0 statement and corresponding BARS.

To promote services to the elderly so that at least 40% of the estimated local population are registered members of the library and 30% are regular users.

BAR Scale for Community Librarian

Contact with Groups
Makes no effort to initiate contact

0 1 2 3 4 5

Has contacted all known established Groups

Investigation of needs and wants
Can only speculate

0 1 2 3 4 5

Has constructed area profile based on available statistics and survey of population

Promotion of Service
Makes no effort to publicise services

0 1 2 3 4 5

Has produced and distributed publicity material directed at user groups

Adjustment of Services
Maintains existing service provision

0 1 2 3 4 5

Has developed new services and activities geared to meet needs

Development of Stock
Revises existing stock

0 1 2 3 4 5

Investigates alternative types of material and purchases to meet known needs and demands

Attitude to users
All users treated alike

0 1 2 3 4 5

Special efforts are made to encourage use by elderly (eg change in seating, large print notices, ease of access, wavering of regulations to allow shopping trolleys)

Staff Training
Branch Staff are trained in routine tasks

0 1 2 3 4 5

Discussions have been held with staff to explore the change emphasis. They are coached on the job and they clearly understand what is expected from them in promoting the services

EXHIBIT 14—GIVING FEEDBACK

Feedback should

1. concentrate on observed behaviour
   —what someone does, not what they are
2. be based on what has been seen by the person giving the feedback not someone else's observation
3. be only given if it is intended to be helpful
4. be informative not advisory
   —the recipient has the choice of what to do with it
5. be given only on areas that the recipient can act upon
   —not things that can not be changed or are outside their control
6. not be overwhelming
   —do not give more than the person can handle and absorb in one go
7. be given in private
8. avoid judgemental, emotive words
9. be given as soon as possible after the behaviour has occurred. Delay long enough for the person to be in a fit state of mind but not too long that they will have forgotten the incident. The giver's state of mind also needs to be considered
10. be given knowing that the recipient can reject it.

EXHIBIT 15—POST-EVENT QUESTIONNAIRE

Training Event

Date

The views of participants in training and development events are needed to ensure the events remain relevant to the needs of staff and the Department and that standards remain high.

Please comment freely as your views will be used to assess the event and to plan future training and development. Use additional paper if you wish. If you wish to remain anonymous leave the last section blank.

1. Why did you participate in the event?
2. What did you expect to gain?
3. What did you learn?
4. What did you *not* learn that you thought you should?
5. Do you think you will be able to apply the learning? (If not, why not?)
6. Were any aspects of the event unhelpful?
7. Are there any related areas in which you would like further training?
8. Are there any other comments you would like to make about this event or your training needs?

Name . . . .   Section . . . .

Date . . . .